JOURNEYING

WITH

THE JESUS PRAYER

JAMES F. WELLINGTON

SLG Press
Convent of the Incarnation
Fairacres, Parker Street
Oxford OX4 1TB
www.slgpress.co.uk

© 2020 SLG Press

First Edition 2020

Fairacres Publications No. 186

Print ISBN 978-0-7283-0031-6
ISSN 0307-1405

James F. Wellington asserts the right to be identified as the author of this work in accordance with the Copyright, Designs and Patents Act 1988.

All rights reserved. No part of this publication may be reproduced, stored in a retrieval system, or transmitted, in any form or by any means, electronic, mechanical, photocopying, recording or otherwise, without the prior permission of the copyright owner.

Edited and typeset in Palatino by Julia Craig-McFeely

Cover image: The Christ Pantocrator of the Deesis mosaic (13th century) in Hagia Sophia (Istanbul, Turkey).

SLG Press
Convent of the Incarnation
Fairacres Oxford
www.slgpress.co.uk
Printed by
Grosvenor Group Ltd, Loughton, Essex

Dedicated to the Community of St John the Baptist, Tolleshunt Knights, where I have learned so much about Orthodoxy and the Jesus Prayer.

CONTENTS

PROLOGUE	1
1 UNCEASING PRAYER	5
2 INNER WATCHFULNESS	11
3 STILLNESS OF HEART	17
4 PERFECT LONGING	23
EPILOGUE	29
BIBLIOGRAPHY	35

PROLOGUE

From the early days following my ordination, I was eager to pursue a more contemplative form of prayer in order to complement the nourishment which I was receiving through the formal structures of the Daily Offices and the Eucharist. In this quest I came across the teaching of the Benedictine monk, John Main. In his book, *Word into Silence*, he advocates a way of Christian meditation which makes use of a prayer-phrase or mantra, whose constant repetition is designed to still the mind and thus open up a route into the silence of God.

Embracing Main's approach, I set about choosing an appropriate prayer-phrase for my contemplation. I had heard of the Jesus Prayer and, though I knew nothing and cared nothing about its background, it seemed to me to be an appropriate wording for the task at hand. 'Lord Jesus Christ, Son of God, have mercy on me', thus became my mantra of choice.

For more than a decade I was using, or rather abusing, the Jesus Prayer in this way. Then in 1995 I read these words of Jean-Claude Barreau, which introduce the Preface to Olivier Clément's *The Roots of Christian Mysticism*: 'Christianity is in the first place an Oriental religion, and it is a mystical religion'.[1] From that point onwards I ceased to regard the Jesus Prayer as a mantra, a mechanism whereby I might enter into the silence of God, and I came to see it as an invocation of the living presence of the Lord Jesus Christ, an invocation rooted in the theology, spirituality and tradition of the Orthodox Church.

This discovery opened up for me a completely different environment from the one with which I was familiar. Until then I had been at ease in the traditions of the Western Church in general and of Anglo-Catholicism in particular. Now, for the first time, the mystical theology of the Desert Fathers and their successors in the Eastern

---

[1] Olivier Clément, *The Roots of Christian Mysticism* (London: New City, 1993), 7.

Church began to speak to me, and I found myself thirsting for a greater knowledge both of the practitioners of the prayer which had come to occupy such a central place in my life with God, and also of the Church which had nurtured them.

In my quest for this greater knowledge I found myself joining the Fellowship of St Alban and St Sergius. I also became a member of the Friends of Mount Athos and, armed with a commendatory note from Bishop (later Metropolitan) Kallistos of Diokleia, I went on pilgrimage to the Holy Mountain, visiting the monasteries of Iveron, Stavronakita, Pantokrator, Vatopeidi and Simonospetra, where I conversed with monks who regularly prayed the Jesus Prayer. In addition, I also embarked upon a regular annual retreat to the Orthodox Monastery of St John the Baptist, Tolleshunt Knights in Essex, where the Jesus Prayer is recited corporately each day.

Furthermore, I eagerly set to the task of studying the literature which bears testimony to the Jesus Prayer's formation and development. I devoured splendid introductions written by authors from England, France and Russia.[2] Inevitably, therefore, I very quickly encountered *The Philokalia*, that great five-volume compendium of the spiritual wisdom of the Greek fathers from the fourth to the fifteenth centuries. *Philokalia* is a Greek word meaning 'love of beauty or goodness' or 'love of beautiful or good things'. The Russian translation of *The Philokalia* is known as the *Dobrotolubiye*. Those who have translated these sacred works into English have rightly stated: 'Indeed although *The Philokalia* is concerned with many other matters, it would not be too much to say that it is the recurrent references to the Jesus Prayer which more than anything else confer on it its inner unity.'[3]

---

[2] From England, Kallistos Ware, *The Power of the Name* (Oxford: SLG Press, 1974); from France, Irénée Hausherr, *The Name of Jesus*, trans. Charles Cummings, Cistercian Studies, 44 (Kalamazoo, MI: Cistercian Publications, 1978); and A Monk of the Eastern Church [Fr Lev Gillet}, *The Jesus Prayer* (New York: St Vladimir's Seminary Press, 1987); from Russia, Ignatius Brianchaninov, *On the Jesus Prayer* (Liberty, TN: St John of Kronstadt Press, 1995); E. Kadloubovsky and Gerald E. H. Palmer, trans., *The Art of Prayer: An Orthodox Anthology* ed. Igumen Chariton of Valamo (London: Faber & Faber, 1966); and Reginald M. French, trans., *The Way of a Pilgrim* (London: SPCK, 1954).

Thus, I endeavoured to move forward in my assimilation of the sacred teaching contained within these writings, firstly through studying the English translations and latterly the Greek texts themselves. In the process of my study and my ongoing prayer life, I found both that the recitation of the Jesus Prayer enhanced my understanding of *The Philokalia*, and that my study of *The Philokalia* deepened my practice and appreciation of the Jesus Prayer. As I have continued along this path, I have been aware of having received a number of graces or gifts from God, which have enhanced my progress.

At the very beginning of this journey the concept of watchfulness *(nepsis)* was, understandably, of great importance to me. The original compilers of *The Philokalia*, St Nikodemos of the Holy Mountain and St Makarios of Corinth, gave to the compendium the title of *The Philokalia of the Neptic Fathers*, thus identifying watchfulness as its most prominent theme. I was soon enthusing about the wisdom to be found in St Hesychios the Priest's text, *On Watchfulness and Holiness*. With this in mind, I came to see that in praying the Jesus Prayer I was guarding my heart and fortifying my inner life against the assaults and provocations of spiritual enemies.

Similarly, it was not very long before I also began to appreciate the significance of inner stillness *(hesychia)* for the ascetical theology which underpinned the various works. Indeed, at this time, my personal discovery of Hesychasm enabled me to move into a new and exciting place in my understanding of contemplation and my life in Christ in general. I came to see the praying of the Jesus Prayer not only as a way of pursuing an inner tranquillity, but also as a way of attaining a concentrated listening and attentiveness *(prosoche)* to the voice of Christ Himself.

Further along my path, assisted by my academic studies, I came to value, in my heart as well as in my mind, the meaning of dispassion or detachment *(apatheia)*. I came to see the praying of the Jesus Prayer as a discipline for controlling the various feelings arising

---

[3] Gerald E. H. Palmer, Philip Sherrard and Kallistos Ware, ed. and trans., *The Philokalia: The Complete Text, compiled by St Nikodimos of the Holy Mountain and St Makarios of Corinth*, i (London: Faber & Faber, 1979), 15.

within me and directing them aright. More positively, the practice empowered me to give pride of place to what a number of the fathers describe as 'purity of heart'.

Again, although penitence and sacramental confession had been an essential part of my life with God for many years, my appreciation of them was further enhanced in my study of the literature surrounding the Jesus Prayer through my discovery of *penthos,* a word meaning sorrow, grief or mourning. Although it is important to understand that 'Lord Jesus Christ, Son of God, have mercy on me' is not solely a penitential prayer, it nevertheless includes a strong element of remorse for personal sin. The *penthos* mentioned by such writers as St Gregory of Sinai and St Gregory Palamas, coupled with references to penitential tears, remind me that sin is a form of death for our life with God, over which we should mourn, but that resurrection comes through the mercy of our Lord Jesus Christ.

Finally, and more recently, I have come to appreciate the crucial role played by intense longing *(pothos)* and deep-seated desire *(eros)* in the heart of the person who feels called to journey with the Jesus Prayer. 'How much do you want it?' is a question which lies behind Jesus' teaching in the parable about the pearl of great price in Matthew 13:45—6. It is surely the key question for anyone who sets out in search of a deeper relationship with God. And, in terms of the wisdom of *The Philokalia,* and with relation to making progress with the Jesus Prayer, it is a matter which encapsulates all of those aspects of the Prayer which are listed above.

Both my recitation of the Prayer and my study of the holy writings have combined to bring me closer to the love of the Most Holy, Blessed and Glorious Trinity. What has led me to write this brief account is the desire to share with others, who already pray the Jesus Prayer, or who would be interested in doing so, a travel narrative which I hope will be of some help to them on their own path. These graces which I have just described, have facilitated the deepening both of my practice of and my delight in a prayer which, like its Author Himself, never ceases to yield priceless treasures to those who are willing to immerse themselves in it.

1
UNCEASING PRAYER

Rejoice always, pray without ceasing.[4]

One of the first books which I read following my Jesus Prayer epiphany in 1995 was *The Way of a Pilgrim*.[5] This anonymous work purports to be a personal account of a nineteenth-century Russian peasant who attends the liturgy in his church, and hears the reading from St Paul's First Letter to the Thessalonians, 'Pray without ceasing'. He tries to understand what these words mean, at first without success.

Then he meets an old monk, an elder, or *staretz* in Russian, who invites him to his monastery. This monk instructs him in the theology and practice of the Jesus Prayer and introduces him to *The Philokalia*. He sets the peasant the task of praying the Jesus Prayer an increasing number of times each day until the Prayer becomes rooted in his heart and mind. Indeed, eventually it is no longer a matter of the peasant saying the Prayer, but rather the Prayer saying itself within him, even to the extent that he finds himself saying the Prayer when he awakes from sleep.

Following the death of his *staretz*, the peasant describes his travels through Russia and Siberia, and, more importantly, his journeying with the Jesus Prayer. On these travels he encounters a whole host of people from various backgrounds. These include a questioning forester, a faithful army officer, a thoughtful schoolmaster, a cynical clerk, a spirited young woman, a generous magistrate with his wife and family, a dutiful maid, a godly blind man, and a devout former naval captain.

In the course of these adventures the peasant is able both to grow in his understanding and practice of the Jesus Prayer, and also to impart the wisdom and knowledge which he has acquired to people who

---

[4] 1 Thess. 5:16–17.
[5] See above, note 2.

are largely eager recipients of what he has to offer to them. Thus, the learner becomes the teacher. Not only does he comprehend the meaning of 'Pray without ceasing'. He also sees it as his calling to share his experience of unceasing interior prayer with those who cross his path. Furthermore, he educates his listeners with regard to the whole spiritual environment of the Prayer. This includes guidance on how they should understand the deeper meaning of the Lord's Prayer, and in what order they should read the works included in *The Philokalia*.

Inevitably, I found myself identifying to some extent with the eponymous Pilgrim. My situation was and is, of course, wholly different from his. He is a solitary figure, while I celebrate the joys of having a wife and a daughter. He is a layman, whereas I am subject to the discipline of the canon law of the Church of England. He had no immediate responsibilities, while I rejoice in those of a husband, a father and a priest.

In addition, without his story, it would not have occurred to me to take literally the Pauline words in 1 Thessalonians 5:17. In the mind-set which dominated so much of my past thinking, I would have written off this kind of interpretation of the sacred text as being unduly fundamentalist, and therefore unworthy of serious consideration. The subtlety of a literal interpretation being capable of conveying something profound would have escaped me.

However, his story touched me deep inside because it connected with my own inner quest to find a different level of prayer from that which was available to me through formal worship, personal intercession or even through the mode of contemplative prayer which I had previously adopted. For that reason, I found myself wanting to pursue with him the meaning of 'Pray without ceasing', and eager to be led by him into a world which was very different from the one with which I had been so familiar for so long.

The teaching which the Pilgrim gives to his attentive listeners stimulated me to reflect more deeply both on biblical texts and also on the writings of the Early Church Fathers. It also assisted me in my approach towards, and in my appreciation of, those works contained within *The Philokalia*.

My first encounter with this compendium came in the form of an anthology translated by E. Kadloubovsky and Gerald Palmer, and published in paperback in 1992.[6] The sequence of works covered in this collection reflects the sequence which the Pilgrim encourages his listeners to follow in order to get the best understanding both of *The Philokalia* and also of the Jesus Prayer itself.

Thus, I was delighted to follow his lead in digesting Nikephoros the Monk, in absorbing St Gregory of Sinai, in sitting at the feet of St Symeon the New Theologian, and in treasuring Sts Kallistos and Ignatios of Xanthopoulos. These became my patristic guides in unceasing prayer, and they were soon to be accompanied by others. I would strongly recommend this anthology as the best starting place for anyone sharing my desire to explore the writings of *The Philokalia* with a view to deepening their understanding of the spiritual environment of the Jesus Prayer.

This desire soon brought me into contact with another significant publication. Not long after my reading of *The Way of a Pilgrim*, I came across a more scholarly tome, written by the Alsatian Jesuit, Irénée Hausherr. The English translation of this work is entitled *The Name of Jesus*.[7] The first part of the book gives an account of the various names used for Jesus in the New Testament and the Early Church Fathers. The second part of the book focuses on the origins of the Jesus Prayer.

Hausherr's basic thesis is that the Jesus Prayer came into being as a result of the same kind of search for unceasing prayer which was carried out by the Russian Pilgrim. This search, however, was performed around fifteen hundred years before that pilgrim was striding along the Russian steppes. And it was initiated by the first generation of monks and nuns in the deserts of Egypt and Palestine.

This particular discovery prompted me to engage with the subject of the Jesus Prayer not simply as a matter of personal devotion, of seeking out that deeper level of prayer pursued by the Pilgrim.

---

[6] E. Kadloubovsky and Gerald E. H. Palmer, trans., *Writings from the Philokalia on Prayer of the Heart* (London: Faber & Faber, 1992).

[7] See above, note 2.

Though this remained my first priority, the Prayer also became for me an object of academic study, which still fascinates and intrigues me more than twenty years on. This study led me to the acquisition of a Lambeth PhD, and the publication of a book based on the doctoral thesis, in which I updated Hausherr's work on the origins of the Prayer in the light of more recent scholarship.[8]

In pursuing this study, I set myself the task of being fed in both heart and mind by this new treasure which God was opening up for me. It was therefore never an option for me to shut myself away in university libraries, while simply analyzing ancient texts. Yes, it was my aim to produce some kind of historical understanding of the *milieu* which gave birth to this pearl of wisdom. However, it was also my aim to do some exploring and questioning within the context of active engagement with those who were themselves practitioners of the Prayer. In this, I hoped to become like the people whom the Pilgrim encountered on his travels, who sat at his feet, and who learned from this master of prayer.

To this end, I went with a fellow priest on pilgrimage to Mount Athos, where we visited five monasteries and participated in their worship. Here I conversed with several monks on their practice and understanding of the Jesus Prayer. A couple of months later, I went on retreat to the Orthodox Monastery of St John the Baptist, in Tolleshunt Knights, a little village near Tiptree in Essex. Here again, I immersed myself in the beauty of the Divine Liturgy and sat at the feet of sages of the Prayer. The insights which I gained, and am still gaining from these adventures, are described more fully in Chapters 2 and 3.

Around this time, I was also greatly blessed in my journeying with the Jesus Prayer through my reading of a further book, entitled *The Art of Prayer: An Orthodox Anthology*.[9] This splendid collection of writings, compiled by the abbot of the Russian monastery of

---

[8] James F. Wellington, *Christe Eleison! The Invocation of Christ in Eastern Monastic Psalmody c.350–450* (Berne: Peter Lang, 2014).

[9] Kadloubovsky and Palmer, *The Art of Prayer*.

Valamo, introduced me to two great nineteenth-century authorities on unceasing prayer, the Russian bishops, St Ignatius Brianchaninov and St Theophan the Recluse. Each of these is a beautiful manifestation of the spirituality which lies behind *The Way of a Pilgrim*.

Of the two, while St Ignatius provides me with important pastoral insights, St Theophan speaks to me more profoundly in terms of his understanding of prayer itself and of the Jesus Prayer in particular. St Theophan defines the essence of inner prayer as 'standing with the mind in the heart before God, either simply living in His presence, or expressing supplication, thanksgiving, and glorification'.[10]

He goes on to describe two forms of this prayer, 'one *strenuous*, when man himself strives for it, and the other *self-impelled*, when prayer exists and acts on its own'. Whereas the former is a product of endeavour, the latter occurs involuntarily, and will do so as a result of the former having attracted the 'mercy of the Lord'.[11] Here we go back to keep company with the Russian Pilgrim, who finds himself saying the Prayer when he awakes from sleep. Somewhat in contrast to the Pilgrim, however, St Theophan insists that, in terms of praying the Jesus Prayer, constant repetition is not required. Instead, he says, 'What is required is a constant aliveness to God—an aliveness present when you talk, read, watch, or examine something'.[12]

St Theophan's teaching on self-impelled or self-acting prayer connects with a quotation from the third-century Alexandrian theologian Origen, which I first came across in Hausherr's book:

> The man who prays continually is the man who combines prayer with necessary works and works with prayer. This is the only way it seems possible to fulfil the precept of unceasing prayer. We have to envision the whole life of a pious Christian as one long prayer, and the exercise we commonly refer to as prayer is merely part of this whole.[13]

---

[10] Ibid., 70–1.
[11] Ibid.
[12] Ibid., 83.
[13] Hausherr, *The Name of Jesus*, 130.

In unceasing prayer, we are not talking about prayer in the conventional sense, that is, the 'strenuous prayer' of St Theophan or the 'exercise we commonly refer to as prayer' in the words of Origen. We are talking about a state rather than an activity. We are talking about becoming prayer rather than offering prayer, in any usual meaning of the term.

Here we find ourselves light years away from the position which I occupied in my initial encounter and usage of the Jesus Prayer. The Jesus Prayer is not a mantra or a device whereby we might enter the stillness of God, even though that is its fruit. It is the constant invocation of God Himself, or the constant remembrance of God, which in itself constitutes unceasing prayer.

This chapter has explored the way in which the Jesus Prayer became the answer to the early monastic quest to fulfil the apostolic command to pray without ceasing. This is how St Theophan describes this process:

> In order to make their thought hold to one thing, the Fathers used to accustom themselves to the continual repetition of a short prayer, and from this habit of constant repetition this small prayer clung to the tongue in such a way that it repeated itself of its own accord. In this manner their thought clung to the prayer and, through the prayer, to the constant remembrance of God. Once this habit has been acquired, the prayer holds us in the remembrance of God, and the remembrance of God holds us in prayer; they mutually support each other. Here, then, is a way of walking before God.[14]

'The prayer holds us in the remembrance of God, and the remembrance of God holds us in prayer'. As I journey with the Jesus Prayer, I find the living out of this truth a constant challenge, and the quest for unceasing prayer a daily struggle. It is to the nature of that struggle that we turn in the next chapter.

---

[14] Kadloubovsky and Palmer, *The Art of Prayer*, 86.

2

INNER WATCHFULNESS

Combine prayer with inner watchfulness, for watchfulness purifies prayer, while prayer purifies watchfulness.[15]

In October 1997, accompanied by the late Canon Desmond Treanor, a priest friend, who shared my devotion to the Jesus Prayer, I made a pilgrimage to Mount Athos. It was a life-changing experience for me, and it ensured that from that time onwards my appreciation of prayer, worship and theology could never be the same again. Such were the blessings which I received on the Holy Mountain.

Located on the Halkidiki peninsular of north-eastern Greece, Mount Athos and its surrounding area is the home to twenty monasteries under the jurisdiction of the Ecumenical Patriarch of Constantinople. It functions as a semi-autonomous monastic republic within the Greek state. The first monastery there was founded by St Athanasios the Athonite in 963. According to legend, the Blessed Virgin Mary was shipwrecked there, and subsequently the Holy Mountain has been dedicated as the Garden of the Mother of God.

After a period of monastic decline in the mid-twentieth century, the arrival of a number of inspiring and charismatic abbots and monks from the 1970s onwards has led to a great revival among its communities. This pilgrimage provided me with the ideal opportunity of conversing with those who were seasoned practitioners of the Jesus Prayer.

As well as three substantial discussions with fathers on the specific subject of the Prayer, and some very useful talks with other monks, my friend and I were privileged to encounter other pilgrims of various nationalities, each one with a most interesting story to tell, and each one eager to hear from us about the current state of Anglican church life. In so many ways, it was a visit which taught me a whole host of lessons about aspects of Christianity of which I was aware,

---

[15] St Philotheos of Sinai, 'Forty Texts on Watchfulness', in Palmer, Sherrard and Ware, *The Philokalia*, iii, 29.

but which had not played as prominent a part as they should have done in my own life of faith.

The sheer beauty of the landscape was in itself an inducement to higher and deeper thinking and praying. One afternoon, at the Monastery of Pantokrator, I sat outside under the autumn sun, reading *The Philokalia*, and I made this note in my travel diary: 'Reading St Maximos the Confessor on the eroticism of God, on a seat overlooking the calm, blue waters of the Aegean, with the green Athonite hills on the other side, and the sun shining brightly, was a very close proximation to my idea of heaven'.

The monastery buildings themselves had their own story to tell about the history of each community. Throughout the centuries, fires have been a regular feature of life in that area, and the longevity or novelty of each structure provided a testimony as to how long it had been since the last great fire in any particular place. Also instructive, though at a much deeper level, was the *skopia* or watchtower, which was often to be found at the landing-stage on the shore near the monastery. No doubt due to the difficult terrain in this part of the Halkidiki peninsular, the founders and builders of the monastic settlements had seen fit to construct their monasteries in places where they were easily accessible from the sea. This meant that fresh provisions could be landed at the community's virtual front door, rather than asking providers to negotiate time-consuming and hazardous tracks over hills and through woods.

However, as the monks were clearly made aware on numerous occasions, easy accessibility is a mixed blessing. The same siting, which facilitated a plentiful traffic of goods and services to the settlements, also provided an opening for a host of less welcome visitors. Like the fires which periodically ravaged the monastic buildings, piracy was also a constant threat to the well-being and even to the survival of the monastic communities. A watchtower was therefore erected at the landing-stage as a form of defence against unwanted intruders. And it was manned in order to safeguard not only the valuable artistic and liturgical artefacts of the monastery but also the very existence of the community itself.

It soon dawned on me, in observing these structures, how magnificently they stood out as a statement of the very *raison-d'être* of all the monasteries on the Holy Mountain and, indeed, of Athonite spirituality itself. This is the spirituality of the Jesus Prayer. This is the spirituality of *The Philokalia of the Neptic Fathers*. This is the way of being a Christian which is rooted in inner watchfulness and attentiveness. This is the way of following Jesus which defines itself in terms of spiritual warfare.

For all those living, dying, waking, sleeping, eating, drinking, worshipping, praying and working in the Athonite monasteries, the real enemy is not the pirate who will come and steal your earthly treasures, or even the pirate who will come and put an end to your earthly life. The real enemy is the pirate who will come and make off with your heavenly riches, and the pirate who will come and steal your soul.

Later on, in the same month, I made a pilgrimage to the Holy Land. In some ways this was a mistake. There was so much from my visit to Mount Athos that I was still trying to assimilate that I inevitably had some difficulty in doing justice to the great treasures which were on offer in Galilee and Jerusalem.

However, the juxtaposition of these two pilgrimages helped me greatly by complementing one another. For, just as my visit to the Holy Land led me to a deeper appreciation of the Gospels in its capacity to give me some kind of reference point for Jesus in His earthly ministry, so my visit to the Holy Mountain led me to a deeper appreciation of the Epistles by giving me a reference point to that whole body of teaching which flows from St Paul's words to the Ephesians: 'For our struggle is not against enemies of blood and flesh, but against the rulers, against the authorities, against the cosmic powers of this present darkness, against spiritual forces of evil in the heavenly places' (Eph. 6:12).

The concept of spiritual warfare is, of course, one which is rooted in the teaching of all churches, of both East and West. As I write these words, I am also approaching my preparation for my sermon for the coming Sunday, the First Sunday of Lent, when we remember Jesus' temptations in the wilderness and His struggle against Satan. And I have always, throughout my entire journey with Jesus, recognized the need for self-examination and the call to guard against evil and to fight valiantly 'against sin, the world and the devil'.

However, my time on Mount Athos, my reflection on the watchtowers, and my immersion in the spiritual environment of the Jesus Prayer and *The Philokalia* have encouraged me to give far greater priority to inner watchfulness both in my practice and in my preaching. A recognition which was once primarily in my head is now gradually becoming more firmly rooted in my heart. There will be more on this in the next chapter.

Again and again, the writers who feature in *The Philokalia* entreat us to use the Jesus Prayer as a form of watchfulness, as a way of guarding the heart, as a means of keeping evil thoughts out of our minds. The Jesus Prayer then becomes for us the equivalent of Jesus' quotations of Scripture to Satan in the wilderness, a way of rebutting the little whispers and promptings which are designed to steer us away from God.

St Hesychios of Sinai cites the Jesus Prayer as a weapon in this unseen warfare. He writes a treatise of texts, *On Watchfulness and Holiness*, to someone called Theodoulos, a 'slave of God'. This is one of the most important works on the Prayer in the whole of *The Philokalia*. He lists four forms of watchfulness, one of which is 'humbly calling on the Lord Jesus Christ for help'. And he says, 'If we have not attained prayer that is free from thoughts, we have no weapon to fight with. By this prayer I mean the prayer which is ever active in the shrine of the soul, and which by invoking Christ scourges and sears our secret enemy'.[16]

Two of the fathers with whom I conversed at some length on the Holy Mountain spoke poignantly about inner watchfulness; although they did not use this precise language, what they were doing was commending the recitation of the Jesus Prayer as a weapon against the demon of pride. For a father in the Monastery of Iveron, unceasing

---

[16] Palmer, Sherrard and Ware, *The Philokalia*, i, 165.

prayer was a means of promoting humility within the heart of the Christian. By affirming our own insignificance, he said, we find our true significance in Christ. For a father in the Monastery of Vatopedi, on the other hand, the focus was more on obedience. Quoting St Ephrem the Syrian of the fourth century, he said, 'Do you think you came to the monastery to pray? No, you came to be obedient!' For both of them, the Jesus Prayer was a sure way of safeguarding the inner shrine of the heart.

The watchtower, of course, was not simply a means whereby the community could remain vigilant against attacks from enemies. It was also a place from which the imminent arrival of welcome visitors could be observed, so that appropriate preparations for their reception could be made. In a similar fashion, inner watchfulness and attentiveness is not only a means of guarding the heart and seeing off the enemy. It is also a way of ensuring that our inner person is in a state of preparedness, so that we are in a position to receive the blessings of Christ. If the former is represented by the season of Lent and Jesus' battle with Satan in the wilderness, the latter is manifested by the season of Advent and the Parable of the Wise and Foolish Bridesmaids.

Another of the writers featured in *The Philokalia*, St Philotheos of Sinai, recognizes the struggle which is involved with maintaining constant vigilance, but he also trumpets the reward for such a state:

> Smoke from wood kindling a fire troubles the eyes; but then the fire gives them light and gladdens them. Similarly, unceasing attentiveness is irksome; but when, invoked in prayer, Jesus draws near, He illumines the heart; for remembrance of Him confers on us spiritual enlightenment and the highest of all blessings.[17]

The word for 'attentiveness' in this passage is *prosoche*, a word almost synonymous with *nepsis*. What St Philotheos is saying here is that inner watchfulness can feel like an arduous process, but if the Christian perseveres with a proper focus, that is with the Jesus Prayer, they can be assured of the light of Christ coming into their heart.

---

[17] Palmer, Sherrard and Ware, *The Philokalia*, ii, 27.

I am greatly inspired but, at the same time, greatly challenged by the Pilgrim's account of his experiences. While he endures physical hardships which, praise God, have not been my lot in life, his progress in his journeying with the Jesus Prayer appears to be on an endless upward curve. He seems to know absolutely nothing of the 'irksome' nature of unceasing prayer and attentiveness, of which St Philotheos writes.

By contrast, this is something that constantly rings true for me in my own journeying with the Prayer. My way of travel has been anything but absolutely smooth. There have been times of great aridity, when Jesus has felt anything but near to me, and when His love, joy and peace have seemed more like intellectual propositions than burning realities within me.

Nevertheless, these periods have been dramatically outshone by those illuminations, those epiphanies, those episodes of enlightenment, when I have known the warmth, the sweetness and the gentleness of my Saviour's presence. The constant and insistent remembrance of Him, in the midst of cloud and darkness, leads us to a blessed assurance that 'the Sun of Righteousness will shine upon us with healing in His wings' (Malachi 4:2).

It is this focus and this assurance which the Jesus Prayer is designed to provide and which, if we persevere with the Prayer in the midst of the dryness, it can deliver for us. Its constant recitation, its unceasing invocation of the Eternal Son of God, is a calling forth in faith of Him of whom St Peter says, 'There is salvation in no one else, for there is no other name under heaven given among mortals by which we must be saved' (Acts 4:12). Guarding the heart against the enemy and keeping our focus on the Lord, the Jesus Prayer is a watchtower in our life of faith.

3

STILLNESS OF HEART

When the heart has acquired stillness it will perceive the heights and depths of knowledge; and the ear of the still intellect will be made to hear marvellous things from God.[18]

Two months after my pilgrimage to the Holy Mountain I made my first visit to the Orthodox Monastery of St John the Baptist, Tolleshunt Knights in Essex. What Mount Athos offered to me on a grand international scale, Tolleshunt Knights provided for me at a more local level, and still does to this day. Founded in 1959 by an Athonite monk, Elder Sophrony, who was canonized in 2019, the monastery from its very beginnings has been a mixed community of monks and nuns of various nationalities.

Worship at the monastery consists of regular Orthodox services, including the Divine Liturgy. However, the feature which most inspired me to make this first visit was the community's practice of praying the Jesus Prayer corporately for two-hour periods each day. This practice consists of a series of individuals, in turn, reciting the Prayer, while the congregation remains in silent contemplation. The language in which the Prayer is prayed varies according to each individual, and may be in English, Greek, Old Church Slavonic, French, German, and so on.

On my first visit to the monastery I was immediately struck by the sense of stillness which prevailed in the chapel during the praying of the Jesus Prayer. Following a short form of Evening Prayer, the lights were dimmed, and within the semi-darkness there followed a gentle, rhythmic invocation in Greek: *Kyrie Iesou Christe, Huie tou Theou, eleison hemas,* 'Lord Jesus Christ, Son of God, have mercy on us'. As I counted off each invocation on the knots of my prayer-rope or *komvoskinion*, I found myself being gently carried along in this flow

---

[18] St Hesychios of Sinai, 'On Watchfulness and Holiness', in Palmer, Sherrard and Ware, *The Philokalia*, i, 132.

of prayer, which, in a strange yet powerful sense, seemed to be moving me both outwardly towards God and inwardly towards myself at the very same time. The fruit of this strange double movement was a deep inner tranquillity which, I came to understand, was described by the Fathers as *hesychia*.

The terms Hesychasm and Hesychasts (those who practice Hesychasm) are historically associated with the revival of mystical prayer on Mount Athos in the fourteenth century. But, as the editors of the English translation of *The Philokalia* point out, they are better applied to the 'whole spiritual tradition going back to the earliest times and delineated in *The Philokalia*'.[19] They also point out that the word *hesychia*, bearing the sense of tranquillity, silence and stillness, is through its Greek root associated with being seated, and therefore concentrated. This is exactly what I encountered in the chapel of St John the Baptist.

Praying the Prayer of Jesus corporately, in the company of people from different parts of the world, rather than privately in the confines of my own home or church, added a different kind of dimension to my journeying. For one thing, there is the obvious point that journeying with the Jesus Prayer is not a solitary endeavour, but something which we embrace as a member of the Body of Christ.

Reading about the Russian Pilgrim in his lonely travels, despite his constant encounters with eager listeners, can give the impression that the Prayer is a private endeavour, an impression which is potentially, at least, conveyed by the title of the book, *The Way of A Pilgrim*. However, nothing could be further from the truth. No form of Christian prayer, whether we are talking about the Jesus Prayer or any other prayer, is prayed in isolation, not even that of a hermit. We pray in solidarity with our brothers and sisters in Christ, who are here in our own country and throughout the whole world, and also in communion with angels and archangels and the whole company of heaven. Whether I am in a chapel with fifty other people or on my own at home, I am praying for the mercy of Jesus in the company of myriads of others.

---

[19] Palmer, Sherrard and Ware, *The Philokalia*, i, 14–15.

For another thing, as I have indicated, this experience of *hesychia* has been of great value to me in trying to make sense of those writings in *The Philokalia* which refer to the 'stillness of heart', or sometimes to the 'stillness of soul', or the 'stillness of mind'. This touches upon two further profound and informative conversations which I had with seasoned practitioners of the Jesus Prayer, one on Mount Athos, and the other at Tolleshunt Knights. Through their wisdom, as well as through my own prayer and reflection, I have been able to place this teaching on *hesychia* and its relationship to the Jesus Prayer in its proper context.

A monk of the Monastery of Simonospetra on Mount Athos spoke to me about praying 'with the mind in the heart'. This is a concept which I had already encountered in my initial study of *The Philokalia* and what it had to say about the Jesus Prayer. The father said that praying with the mind in the heart could only be done with the grace of God. The natural situation for the mind is to be in the heart. This was the natural situation for Adam before the Fall, when he was a united personality. Our situation as fallen people means that there is a disjunction between mind and heart. Therefore, the role of the Jesus Prayer, also called the 'prayer of the heart', is to unify the mind and the heart.

A monk of the Monastery of St John the Baptist, Tolleshunt Knights, was keen to insist that the therapeutic metaphor was as much part of Christian tradition as the military metaphor. He spoke of invoking the 'therapeutic name of Jesus'. He said that in the modern age, and especially in the West, there has been a separation of heart and mind, producing materialism, sentimentalism, reactions and counter-reactions. This has resulted in a loss of wholeness. In the Hesychast way, however, we find things back in their original place as part of the whole. This is what happens when we use therapy. The Jesus Prayer, as a spiritual remedy which restores the union of heart and mind, provides this therapy. It is about purification, illumination and glorification.

At this point, it is probably of some help to the reader to explain precisely what is meant by 'heart' in the present discussion. The editors of the English translation of *The Philokalia* provide us with an excellent working definition. They say that the heart or *kardia* in the Greek is:

> ... not simply the physical organ but the spiritual centre of man's being, man as made in the image of God, his deepest and truest self, or the inner shrine, to be entered only through sacrifice and death, in which the mystery of the union between the divine and the human is consummated. '"I called with my whole heart", says the psalmist, that is, with body, soul and spirit' (John Klimakos, *The Ladder of Divine Ascent*, Step 28, translated by Archimandrite Lazarus [London, 1959], 257–8). 'Heart' has therefore an all-embracing significance: 'prayer of the heart' means prayer not just of the emotions and affections, but of the whole person, including the body.[20]

How does the Jesus Prayer heal our divided heart and mind? The answer inevitably is to be found in *The Philokalia*. In the fourth volume there is a work, referred to in *The Way of a Pilgrim*, attributed to St Symeon the New Theologian, a tenth-century monk, who is one of the most revered mystic authorities in the Orthodox Church. According to *Three Methods of Prayer*, there are two ways of contemplative prayer which are to be avoided and one which is to be embraced. This third way includes some instruction on bodily posture and breathing technique, but the core of the teaching is as follows:

> [S]earch inside yourself with your intellect so as to find the place of the heart, where all the powers of the soul reside. To start with you will find there darkness and impenetrable density. Later, when you persist and practice this task day and night, you will find, as though miraculously, an unceasing joy. For as soon as the intellect attains the place of the heart, at once it sees things of which it previously knew nothing. It sees the open space within the heart and it beholds itself as entirely luminous and full of discrimination. From then on, from whatever side a distractive thought may appear, before it has come to completion and assumed a form, the intellect immediately drives it away and destroys it with the invocation of Jesus Christ.[21]

---

[20] Palmer, Sherrard and Ware, *The Philokalia*, i, 361–2.
[21] Palmer, Sherrard and Ware, *The Philokalia*, iv, 72–3.

This repositioning of the intellect within the heart is also described by Nikephoros the Monk in *On Watchfulness and Guarding the Heart* in the same volume of *The Philokalia*.[22] This indicates how the attainment of *hesychia*, the stillness of heart, is inextricably linked with inner watchfulness and attentiveness. Only when my inner watchfulness and attentiveness have safeguarded my heart, the inner core of my being, from unruly thoughts and distractions can my mind find that open space to occupy and be reunited with my heart in deep-seated tranquillity.

St Theophan the Recluse, whom we met in Chapter 1, also had much to say about the union of the heart and mind. Like most Russian mystics, he was deeply sceptical about any prescription of bodily performance relating to the Jesus Prayer, such as those involving posture and breathing. He saw these as a distraction from the core of the Prayer itself and also as dangerous in some circumstances. Personally, I share his scepticism and, for that reason, am happy to omit from this book the section from *Three Methods of Prayer* which describes the psychosomatic technique advocated by its author.

Writing to one of his many spiritual children, St Theophan presents the union of heart and mind in this very simple way:

> You ask what it means, to be with the mind in the heart? It means this. You know where the heart is? How can you help knowing it having once learnt? Then stand there with attention and remain steadfastly within, and you will have your mind in your heart. The mind is inseparable from attention; where one is there will be the other.[23]

From all that has been said, it is evident that it is extremely difficult to find the words which are capable of capturing such an interior exercise as placing the mind within the heart. St Theophan's words, 'Then stand there with attention and remain steadfastly within' is probably the nearest we can get to the essence of the practice. None of the fathers who write on the Jesus Prayer seek to minimize this

---

[22] Ibid., 204–6.
[23] Kadloubovsky and Palmer, *The Art of Prayer*, 189.

difficulty. However, in terms of the practice itself, it is clear that the praying of the Jesus Prayer, faithfully and constantly, enables us to find that inner watchfulness and attentiveness which can lead us to the *hesychia*, the stillness of heart, of which the fathers write.

In endeavouring to formulate an exposition of this teaching in my own journeying with the Jesus Prayer, I find myself returning to my own experience of the corporate prayer at Tolleshunt Knights, which, indeed, has done so much to aid and inspire my practice of the Prayer. And I come back to what I have described as that strange and powerful double-movement, which seemed to be moving me both outwardly towards God and inwardly towards myself at the very same time.

There is, of course, a biblical text, greatly loved by all mystics and monastics, and indeed treasured by those who feel drawn to contemplative prayer in whatever form, which helps me to make some kind of sense of the experience which I have described. This is where Jesus says to the Pharisees, 'The kingdom of God is not coming with things that can be observed; nor will they say, "Look, here it is!" or "There it is!" For, in fact, the kingdom of God is within you' (Luke 17:20–1). In our contemplation, in our journeying with the Jesus Prayer, we are drawn to the God who both infinitely transcends us and yet, at the same time, lives within the depths of our hearts. The next question is, 'Exactly how much do we want to be drawn to Him?'

4

PERFECT LONGING

This is one of the outer passions and it stays with you because you still have not acquired a perfect longing for God.[24]

From the very beginning of the journey which I have been describing, in the process of my study and my ongoing prayer life, I found both that my praying of the Jesus Prayer enhanced my understanding of *The Philokalia*, and that at the same time my study of *The Philokalia* deepened my practice and appreciation of the Jesus Prayer. In this way I was able to experience something of the coming together of heart and mind which I explored in the previous chapter, and to see my journey holistically in terms of both devotional and intellectual development.

One of the key resources for this progression has been an anonymous work included in the second volume of *The Philokalia*. Both the authorship and the dating of *A Discourse on Abba Philemon* is unclear. Nevertheless, the editors of the English translation suggest that the eponymous character lived in Egypt in the sixth century or, at the latest, prior to the Arab conquest of the seventh century.[25] Though this is highly hypothetical, if there is some accuracy in the recorded words of the abba in question, this text could provide the earliest known version of what was to become the classical expression of the Jesus Prayer, 'Lord Jesus Christ, Son of God, have mercy on me'.

For this reason, I took a special interest in the *Discourse* and studied the work closely. It greatly assisted me in formulating my doctoral thesis on the origins of the Jesus Prayer, which was based on an analysis of the close relationship between psalmody and contemplative prayer in the practice of early Eastern monasticism. Here I had come across one of the 'founding documents' of the Jesus Prayer,

---

[24] 'A Discourse on Abba Philemon', in Palmer, Sherrard and Ware, *The Philokalia*, ii, 347.

[25] Palmer, Sherrard and Ware, *The Philokalia*, ii, 343.

which in almost the same breath praises God who has 'impressed the power of the psalms on my poor soul as He did on the soul of the prophet David'.[26]

It was much later, however, while I was pursuing another academic interest, that a different passage in the *Discourse* spoke to me and provided me with a new channel for reflecting on the Jesus Prayer. This new academic interest featured the mystical theology of St Gregory of Nyssa, a fourth-century writer whose insights I have come to admire and assimilate in great measure.

In his *Homilies on the Song of Songs*, St Gregory writes about the Bride passionately pursuing her Bridegroom. And he makes this statement about the two Greek words most commonly used for 'love' in the ancient world, *agape* and *eros*: 'She, then, who has put the veil off from her eyes sees the unspeakable beauty of the Bridegroom with a pure eye and in this way is wounded by the incorporeal and fiery arrow of love, for *agape* when intensified is called *eros*'.[27]

The use of the word *eros* for 'love' would have been controversial in Christian circles in St Gregory's day, given its associations with pagan deities and with, to put it mildly, highly questionable forms of sexual conduct. The bishop of Nyssa, however, is trying to promote among his readers an intensity in their love for God which, clearly, he does not feel is fully expressed in the conventional New Testament word for 'love', *agape*. Thus, not only in his commentary on the Song of Songs, but also in many of his other works, he uses the word *eros* and another word *pothos*, which like *eros* is also the name of a pagan love-god, to convey the intensity of the love, longing and desire for God which he is encouraging in the hearts of his audience.

My studies of St Gregory of Nyssa led me to revisit the writings of *The Philokalia*. What I discovered in this revisitation was a modest but significant use of the words *eros* and, to a lesser extent, *pothos*

---

[26] Ibid., 347.
[27] Richard A. Norris Jr., *Gregory of Nyssa: Homilies on the Song of Songs* (Atlanta: Society of Biblical Literature, 2012), 403.

along the same lines in which they are used in St Gregory's works. Indeed, the editors of the English translation include *eros* among the words listed in the Glossary, and translate it as 'intense longing'.

From this research, it is clear that the writers of many of the works in *The Philokalia*, the compendium whose inner unity is conferred by the recurrent references to the Jesus Prayer, have followed St Gregory of Nyssa in choosing to use problematic words in order to convey the sheer power and force of the devotion to God which they see as essential for any progress in the monastic life in particular and the Christian life in general.

The roll-call of sages who employ these words is staggering. And they include some of those who have important things to say about the Jesus Prayer, such as St Hesychios the Priest, St Diadochos of Photike, St Gregory of Sinai, St Gregory Palamas, and Sts Kallistos and Ignatios Xanthopoulos. They also include the writer of *A Discourse on Abba Philemon*. In this work we find the following passage:

> A brother named John came from the coast to Father Philemon and, clasping his feet, said to him: 'What shall I do to be saved? For my intellect vacillates to and fro and strays after all the wrong things'. After a pause, the father replied: 'This is one of the outer passions and it stays with you because you still have not acquired a perfect longing *(teleion pothon)* for God. The warmth of this longing and of the knowledge of God has not yet come to you'. The brother said to him: 'What shall I do, father?' Abba Philemon replied: 'Meditate inwardly for a while, deep in your heart; for this can cleanse your intellect of these things'. The brother, not understanding what was said, asked the Elder: 'What is inward meditation, father?' The Elder replied: 'Keep watch in your heart; and with watchfulness say in your mind with awe and trembling: "Lord Jesus Christ, have mercy upon me". For this is the advice which the blessed Diadochos gave to beginners'.[28]

The brother's initial spiritual difficulties arise from the fact that he lacks this 'perfect longing'. Whatever desire or yearning for God he may have in his heart, it is insufficiently warm to enable him to

---

[28] Palmer, Sherrard and Ware, *The Philokalia*, ii, 347.

progress in his knowledge of the One to whom he prays. The longing which occupies his heart appears to be at best lukewarm, like the works of the Church of Laodicea in Revelation 3:16. Without this 'perfect longing' he will continue to be thwarted in his endeavours to arrive at a deeper relationship with God.

The father diagnoses the brother's ailment but stops there, silently encouraging the brother to question him further regarding his analysis. And, in response to the brother's subsequent enquiry, Abba Philemon prescribes inward meditation, deep within the heart, or what future generations will term the 'prayer of the heart' or the Jesus Prayer. This is the practice which will warm the brother's heart and which will enable him to find that 'perfect longing for God', which he currently lacks.

It is clear, therefore, that the Jesus Prayer is not only a vehicle for unceasing prayer, not only a channel for inner watchfulness and attentiveness, and not only an agent for the stillness of heart. It is also a means by which those who are seeking a closer walk with Jesus may achieve a perfect longing, an intensity of love and desire for God and for the things of God. It is an instrument whereby the Bride of Christ can be inflamed with passion for her divine Bridegroom, the holy object of her desire.

In different areas of life it is easy to see how desire can often be the key factor which determines either success or failure. A marriage, or some other family connection or a friendship, may have hit the rocks. Whether or not such a relationship survives will depend upon a whole host of things, not least on the desire of both parties to make it work. A person's application for promotion at work will involve scrutiny of their past performance and presentation of their future aims. Whether or not they are preferred for the job over another person with similar qualifications may well come down to how badly they want it. Two football teams may be equally matched in skills on the pitch. The question as to which one will emerge on top may well be answered, the one that desires the victory more than the other.

This is undoubtedly true with regard to progress in the life of faith. 'How much do I want it?' is a question which every Christian who seeks a deeper life with God needs to ask himself or herself. As I continue on my journey with the Jesus Prayer, I am constantly aware of the hard sayings of Jesus to one who said, 'Lord, first let me go and bury my father', and to another who said 'Let me first say farewell to those at my home' (Luke 9:59–62). And even if I create some wiggle-room for myself in order to escape the severity of the literal interpretations, I am still left with the continual challenge of the exacting question, 'Exactly how much do I want to carry on walking along this road?'

Mercifully, the answer to that question does not rest with myself alone. If it did, I have no doubt that my journeying with the Jesus Prayer and my determination to find a closer walk with God would have ended long ago. St Gregory of Sinai sees the Jesus Prayer as a way of renewing the grace which every Christian receives at his or her baptism. On that day we are incorporated into a Spirit-filled Body which continues to feed and nurture us, despite our weaknesses. The grace which we receive on that day is constantly renewed by that same Spirit, who is always working alongside us and within us, always eliciting our co-operation, to create a synergy which empowers and enables us to grow in that grace.

Renewal comes in many forms, including the sacraments of the Church, the study of the word of God and of the lives and teachings of the Saints, private prayer and public worship, and the fellowship of other Christians. The Jesus Prayer itself renews us from within, because we are carried along by the action of God within us, as much as by our own strivings. Inspired by the words of Abba Philemon, and further motivated by St Gregory of Nyssa's account of the Bride's relentless reaching out towards her Bridegroom, I have come to see the Jesus Prayer as, among other things, a lover's constant cry to their beloved. For me, it is an expression of an intense love, a perfect longing, for Jesus. It is an endless reaching out in love, a continual straining forward for the heavenly goal (Phil. 3:13–14), that is, Christ our God.

It is also an unceasing prayer for, and an unceasing pursuit of, the many mercies or blessings which Jesus showers upon those who seek Him. Such mercies include healing and forgiveness, compassion and assurance, love, joy and peace. As I have discovered in my journeying, this unceasing pursuit does not end in frustration, as one might expect. On the contrary, it energizes the pursuer as Jesus, the object of our longing, draws us further into His stillness.

In being the means by which those who are seeking a closer walk with Jesus may achieve a perfect longing for God, the Jesus Prayer underpins the other blessings which we have explored in the previous chapters. For this is the perfect longing to be with God, and to enjoy His company, ceaselessly in prayer. This is the intense desire to safeguard the treasures of our life with God, and at the same time to be prepared for Him drawing near to us, through inner watchfulness and attentiveness. This is the passionate yearning for the stillness of both heart and mind and a return to something approaching the beauty of Eden. The constant invocation of Christ and His mercy warms the heart and places us in the environment where we can enjoy these divine treasures.

EPILOGUE

Some years ago, in an address to the clergy of the Diocese of Southwell and Nottingham, the former Archbishop of Canterbury, Lord Rowan Williams, said that prayer is not so much about acquiring a skill as entering an environment. How true his words are in relation to the Jesus Prayer! Through praying the Prayer we enter God's environment. We expose ourselves to His tender love and mercy. We open up our hearts to Him.

In my journeying with the Jesus Prayer, I have found myself entering two environments, of both of which I was aware, to some extent, but neither of which I knew particularly well. As a result of my travels, I can honestly say that, while I possess nothing like a complete knowledge of either of them, nevertheless, I know a good deal more about both of them than I did when I first embarked on my journey.

The first environment consists of the entire milieu of the Orthodox Church, its history, its beliefs, its theology, its spirituality, its liturgy, and its Saints. Prior to my epiphany, in my Western ignorance I had regarded Orthodoxy as something 'weird and wonderful', indeed as something fascinating, but certainly not as something that should be taken too seriously at either an intellectual or a spiritual level.

However, the grace and mercy of God have led me away from such witlessness and arrogance and opened up for me an Aladdin's Cave of riches beyond my wildest imagination. My eyes have been opened to ways of looking at God, at myself, and at the world, which would have remained hidden from me had it not been for that divine epiphany in 1995.

As a result of that revelation, I was put in touch with an entire tradition which completely reshaped my thinking and my praying. I was allowed access to authorities, both ancient and modern, at whose wells I have been privileged to drink for a quarter of a century. And the wonderful thing about these wells is that they never seem to run dry. Like the Jesus Prayer itself, they are like fountains which keep on delivering an endless flow of living water. While I have chosen to remain a loyal son of the Church of England, I am greatly indebted to a host of Orthodox writers, bishops, priests, monks, nuns and lay people, who have so graciously granted me both their generous hospitality and their wisdom.

The second environment which I have entered in my journeying with the Jesus Prayer is what the Isley Brothers sang about way back in 1968, 'This Old Heart of Mine'. It is true that, in some senses, religious quests, beliefs and practices can degenerate into a damaging and dangerous introspection where the believer can be led astray into a variety of forms of egocentrism. This temptation is clearly to be counted among the many enemies which the inner watchfulness associated with the spirituality of the Jesus Prayer is designed to combat. The accusation of 'navel-gazing', in a pejorative sense, is wholly justified where the focus of attention is on the self, rather than on the God who is to be encountered and adored at the centre of the self, that is, in the heart.

However, anyone embarking on any form of contemplative prayer, with its vocation to see God in all things and to see all things in God, has to take seriously the mystical interpretation of the words of Jesus in Luke 17:20–1:

> Being asked by the Pharisees when the kingdom of God was coming, he answered them, "The kingdom of God is not coming with signs to be observed; nor will they say, 'Lo, here it is!' or 'There!' for behold, the kingdom of God is in the midst of you."

For the witness of mystics throughout the ages, those from all traditions who have claimed to have had experiences of the immediacy of God, will testify that the great part of the search for God lies in the journey inwards.

It is here that the language about 'entering an environment' begins to creak a little. Towards the end of my travel diary on Mount Athos I recalled our experience when we arrived at the port of

Daphne, ready for our departure. I noted that the officials searched our rucksacks to make sure we were not stealing any treasures from the Holy Mountain. Then I wrote with a flourish, 'The truth is, however, that we were indeed taking away with us the real treasures of the Holy Mountain, treasures imprinted in our hearts and minds'.

It was only some years later that I came to understand the superficiality of that comment. Strictly speaking, we were not taking treasures away with us. We had brought them with us, that is, the hearts in which God was pleased to dwell, and in which He was always longing to be discovered, worshipped and obeyed. While I have been entering a new environment in journeying with the Jesus Prayer, the environment of the heart, it is also true to say that I have been in the process of understanding more and more about the environment in which I already live and move and have my being.

One of the practitioners of the Jesus Prayer whom I encountered was a monk who lived in Shropshire. He spoke to me about what I can only describe as the inner geography of the heart. The heart, he said, is the centre of our being, a sanctuary where God and the human creature meet. He used the analogy of a church building. The heart, he said, is the altar or sanctuary. The mind is the nave. The body is the narthex or outer part of the church. We need to draw all our faculties together in our heart, like drawing a family together to meet the royal visitor.

This echoes the four themes explored in this book. Firstly, we have seen how the Jesus Prayer, as unceasing prayer, is rightly described as the 'prayer of the heart'. It moves beyond the prayer of the lips and the prayer of the mind because it emerges from the heart, from the centre of our being. Secondly, as a weapon in spiritual warfare, the Prayer is an important means of guarding the heart, of keeping it free, not only from evil thoughts, but from all kinds of distractions which can impede prayer. Also, while closing the heart to what is evil, it functions as a way of keeping the heart open to what is good; that is, open to God and to the things of God. Thirdly, through keeping the heart closed to what is evil and open to what is good, the Prayer leads us to stillness of heart, where we can rest in the sublime tranquillity of Love Divine. Fourthly, by providing us with a constant invocation of our heavenly Bridegroom, the Prayer warms the heart, and drives us on to an intense love, longing and desire for Him who is the Author of our salvation.

The heart is the environment where we meet God, where He is to be found, loved, longed-for and desired. It is not for nothing that the Jesus Prayer is described as the 'prayer of the heart', because, for so many people, it is the means by which we can open ourselves up to God, and be opened up by God, so that we can draw close to Him. As I have indicated, for me this process, this journeying, this drawing close to God, this exploration of my inner geography, is very much a work in progress. I travel on in faith, hope and love, continuing to learn about my heart and, I hope, continuing to learn about the God who longs to meet me there.

Lord Jesus Christ, Son of God, have mercy on me.

BIBLIOGRAPHY

Ignatius Brianchaninov, *On the Jesus Prayer* (Liberty TN: St John of Kronstadt Press, 1995).

Olivier Clément, *The Roots of Christian Mysticism* (London: New City, 1993).

Reginald M. French, trans., *The Way of a Pilgrim* (London: SPCK, 1954).

A Monk of the Eastern Church [Fr Lev Gillet], *The Jesus Prayer* (Crestwood NY: St Vladimir's Seminary Press, 1987).

Irénée Hausherr, *The Name of Jesus*, trans. Charles Cummings, Cistercian Studies, 44 (Kalamazoo MI: Cistercian Publications, 1978).

E. Kadloubovsky and Gerald E. H. Palmer, trans., *The Art of Prayer: An Orthodox Anthology*, ed. Chariton of Valamo (London: Faber & Faber, 1966).

E. Kadloubovsky and Gerald E. H. Palmer, trans., *Writings from The Philokalia on the Prayer of the Heart* (London: Faber & Faber, 1992).

Richard A. Norris Jr (trans.), *Gregory of Nyssa: Homilies on the Song of Songs* (Atlanta: Society of Biblical Literature, 2012).

Gerald E. H. Palmer, Philip Sherrard, and Kallistos Ware, ed. and trans., *The Philokalia: The Complete Text, compiled by St Nikodimos of the Holy Mountain and St Makarios of Corinth*, vol. 1 (London: Faber & Faber, 1979).

_____ vol. 2 (London: Faber & Faber, 1984).

_____ vol. 3 (London: Faber & Faber, 1984).

_____ vol. 4 (London: Faber & Faber, 1995).

St. George Monastery, Jerusalem, *The Philokalia: The Complete Text, compiled by St Nikodimos of the Holy Mountain and St Makarios of Corinth*, vol. 5 (Oceanitissa [Electronic publication (kindle)] June 30, 2020, print version forthcoming).

Kallistos Ware, *The Power of the Name* (Oxford: SLG Press, 1974).

James F. Wellington, *Christe Eleison! The Invocation of Christ in Eastern Monastic Psalmody c.350–450* (Berne: Peter Lang, 2014).

_____ *Praying the Psalms with Jesus: A Journey of Discovery and Recognition* (Cambridge: Grove Books, 2015).

_____ *Beguiled by Jesus: Faith and the Language of Intimacy* (Cambridge: Grove Books, 2017).

SLG PRESS PUBLICATIONS

FP001	*Prayer and the Life of Reconciliation*	Gilbert Shaw (1969)
FP002	*Aloneness Not Loneliness*	Mother Mary Clare SLG (1969)
FP004	*Intercession*	Mother Mary Clare SLG (1969)
FP008	*Prayer: Extracts from the Teaching of Fr Gilbert Shaw* Gilbert Shaw (1973)
FP012	*Learning to Pray*	Mother Mary Clare SLG (1970)
FP015	*Death, the Gateway to Life*	Gilbert Shaw (1971)
FP016	*The Victory of the Cross*	Dumitru Stăniloae (1970)
FP026	*The Message of Saint Seraphim*	Irina Gorainov (1974)
FP028	*Julian of Norwich: Four Studies to Commemorate the sixth Centenary of the Revelations of Divine Love*
	Sr Benedicta Ward SLG, Sr Eileen Mary SLG (1973), ed. A. M. Allchin
FP043	*The Power of the Name: The Jesus Prayer in Orthodox Spirituality*
		Kallistos Ware (1974)
FP046	*Prayer and Contemplation and Distractions are for Healing*
		Robert Llewelyn (1975)
FP048	*The Wisdom of the Desert Fathers* trans. Sr Benedicta Ward SLG (1975)
FP050	*Letters of Saint Antony the Great*	trans. Derwas Chitty (1975)
FP054	*From Loneliness to Solitude*	Roland Walls (1976)
FP055	*Theology and Spirituality*	Andrew Louth (1976, rev. 1978)
FP061	*Kabir: The Way of Love and Paradox*	Sr Rosemary SLG (1977)
FP062	*Anselm of Canterbury: A Monastic Scholar*
		Sr Benedicta Ward SLG (1973)
FP067	*Mary and the Mystery of the Incarnation: An Essay on the Mother of God in the Theology of Karl Barth*	Andrew Louth (1977)
FP068	*Trinity and Incarnation in Anglican Tradition*	A. M. Allchin (1977)
FP070	*Facing Depression*	Gonville ffrench-Beytagh (1978)
FP071	*The Single Person*	Philip Welsh (1979)
FP072	*The Letters of Ammonas, Successor of St Antony*
		trans. Derwas Chitty (1979)
FP074	*George Herbert, Priest and Poet*	Kenneth Mason (1980)
FP075	*A Study of Wisdom: Three Tracts by the Author of The Cloud of Unknowing*	trans. Clifton Wolters (1980)
FP078	*Silence in Prayer and Action*	Sr Edmée SLG (1981)
FP081	*The Psalms: Prayer Book of the Bible*
	Dietrich Bonhoeffer, trans. Sr Isabel SLG (1982)
FP082	*Prayer and Holiness*	Dumitru Stăniloae (1982)
FP085	*Eight Chapters on Perfection and Angels' Song*
	Walter Hilton, trans. Rosemary Dorward (1983)

FP088	*Creative Suffering*	Iulia de Beausobre
FP090	*Bringing Forth Christ: Five Feasts of the Child Jesus by St Bonaventure*	
		trans. Eric Doyle OFM (1984)
FP092	*Gentleness in John of the Cross*	Thomas Kane (1985)
FP093	*Prayer: The Work of the Spirit*	Sr Edmée SLG (1985)
FP094	*Saint Gregory Nazianzen: Selected Poems*	trans. John McGuckin (1986)
FP095	*The World of the Desert Fathers: Stories & Sayings from the Anonymous Series of the 'Apophthegmata Patrum'*	
		trans. Columba Stewart OSB (1986)
FP101	*Anglicanism: A Canterbury Essay*	Kenneth Mason (1987)
FP104	*Growing Old With God*	T. N. Rudd (1988)
FP105	*The Simplicity of Prayer: Extracts from the teaching of Mother Mary Clare SLG*	Mother Mary Clare SLG (1988)
FP106	*Julian Reconsidered*	Kenneth Leech, Sr Benedicta SLG (1988)
FP108	*The Unicorn: Meditations on the Love of God*	
		Harry Galbraith Miller (1989)
FP109	*The Creativity of Diminishment*	Sister Anke (1990)
FP111	*A Kind of Watershed: An Anglican Lay View of Sacramental Confession*	
		Christine North (1990)
FP116	*Jesus, the Living Lord*	Bp Michael Ramsey (1992)
FP117	*The Spirituality of Saint Cuthbert*	Sr Benedicta Ward SLG (1992)
FP120	*The Monastic Letters of St Athanasius the Great*	
		trans. Leslie Barnard (1994)
FP122	*The Hidden Joy*	Sr Jane SLG, ed. Dorothy Sutherland (1994)
FP123	*At the Lighting of the Lamps: Hymns of the Ancient Church*	
		trans. John McGuckin (1995)
FP124	*Prayer of the Heart: An Approach to Silent Prayer and Prayer in the Night*	
		Alexander Ryrie (1995)
FP125	*Whole Christ: The Spirituality of Ministry*	Philip Seddon (1996)
FP063	*Evelyn Underhill, Anglican Mystic: Two Centenary Essays*	
		A. M. Allchin, Bp Michael Ramsey
FP127	*Apostolate and the Mirrors of Paradox*	
		Sydney Evans, ed. Andrew Linzey, Brian Horne (1996)
FP128	*The Wisdom of Saint Isaac the Syrian*	Sebastian Brock (1997)
FP129	*Saint Thérèse of Lisieux: Her Relevance for Today*	
		Sr Eileen Mary SLG (1997)
FP130	*Expectations: Five Addresses for Those Beginning Ministry*	Sr Edmée SLG
FP131	*Scenes from Animal Life: Fables for the Enneagram Types*	
		Waltraud Kirschke, trans. Sr Isabel SLG (1998)
FP132	*Praying the Word of God: The Use of Lectio Divina*	
		Charles Dumont OCSO (1999)

FP134	*The Hidden Way of Love: Jean-Pierre de Caussade's Spirituality of Abandonment*	Barry Conaway (1999)
FP135	*Shepherd and Servant: The Spiritual Theology of Saint Dunstan*	Douglas Dales (2000)
FP136	*Eternity and Time*	Dumitru Stăniloae, trans. A. M. Allchin (2001)
FP137	*Pilgrimage of the Heart*	Sr Benedicta Ward SLG (2001)
FP138	*Mixed Life*	Walter Hilton, trans. Rosemary Dorward (2001)
FP140	*A Great Joy: Reflections on the Meaning of Christmas*	Kenneth Mason (2001)
FP141	*Bede and the Psalter*	Sr Benedicta Ward SLG (2002)
FP142	*Abhishiktananda: A Memoir of Dom Henri Le Saux*	Murray Rogers, David Barton (2003)
FP143	*Friendship in God: The Encounter of Evelyn Underhill & Sorella Maria of Campello*	A. M. Allchin (2003)
FP144	*Christian Imagination in Poetry and Polity: Some Anglican Voices from Temple to Herbert.*	Archbishop Rowan Williams (2004)
FP145	*The Reflections of Abba Zosimas, Monk of the Palestinian Desert*	trans. John Chryssavgis (2004)
FP146	*The Gift of Theology: The Trinitarian Vision of Ann Griffiths and Elizabeth of Dijon*	A. M. Allchin (2005)
FP147	*Sacrifice and Spirit*	Bp Michael Ramsey (2005)
FP148	*Saint John Cassian on Prayer*	trans. A. M Casiday (2006)
FP149	*Hymns of Saint Ephrem the Syrian*	trans. Mary Hansbury (2006)
FP150	*Suffering: Why all this suffering? What do I do about it?*	Reinhard Körner OCD, trans. Sr Avis Mary SLG (2006)
FP151	*A True Easter: The Synod of Whitby 664 AD*	Sr Benedicta Ward SLG (2007)
FP152	*Prayer as Self-offering*	Alexander Ryrie (2007)
FP153	*From Perfection to the Elixir: How George Herbert Fashioned a Famous Poem*	Ben de la Mare (2008)
FP154	*The Jesus Prayer: Gospel Soundings*	Sr Pauline Margaret CHN (2008)
FP155	*Loving God Whatever: Through the Year with Sister Jane*	Sister Jane SLG (2006)
FP156	*Prayer and Meditation for a Sleepless Night*	(1993)
FP157	*Being There: Caring for the Bereaved*	John Porter (2009)
FP158	*Learn to Be at Peace: The Practice of Stillness*	Andrew Norman (2010)
FP159	*From Holy Week to Easter*	George Pattison (2010)
FP160	*Strength in Weakness: The Scandal of the Cross*	John W. Rogerson (2010)
FP161	*Augustine Baker: Frontiers of the Spirit*	Victor de Waal (2010)

FP162	*Out of the Depths*	
	Gonville ffrench-Beytagh; epilogue Wendy Robinson (1990)	
FP163	*God and Darkness: A Carmelite Perspective*	
	Gemma Hinricher OCD,trans. Sr Avis Mary SLG (2010)	
FP164	*The Gift of Joy*	Curtis Almquist SSJE (2011)
FP165	*'I Have Called You Friends': Suggestions for the Spiritual Life based on the Farewell Discourses of Jesus*	Reinhard Körner OCD (2012)
FP166	*Leisure*	Mother Mary Clare SLG (2012)
FP167	*Carmelite Ascent: An Introduction to St Teresa and St John of the Cross*	Mother Mary Clare SLG (1973)
FP168	*Ann Griffiths and Her Writings*	Llewellyn Cumings (2012)
FP169	*The Our Father*	Sr Benedicta Ward SLG (2012)
FP170	*Exploring Silence*	Wendy Robinson (1974, 3/2013)
FP171	*The Spiritual Wisdom of the Syriac Book of Steps*	Robert A Kitchen (2013)
FP172	*The Prayer of Silence*	Alexander Ryrie (2012)
FP173	*On Tour in Byzantium: Excerpts from The Spiritual Meadow of John Moschus*	Ralph Martin SSM (2013)
FP174	*Monastic Life*	Bonnie Thurston (2016)
FP175	*Shall All Be Well? Reflections for Holy Week*	Graham Ward (2015)
FP176	*Solitude and Communion: Papers on the Hermit Life*	ed. A. M. Allchin
FP177	*The Prayers of Jacob of Serugh*	ed. Mary Hansbury (2015)
FP178	*The Monastic Hours of Prayer*	Sr Benedicta Ward SLG (2016)
FP179	*The Desert of the Heart: Daily Readings with the Desert Fathers*	trans. Sr Benedicta Ward SLG (2016)
FP180	*In Company with Christ: Lent, Palm Sunday, Good Friday & Easter to Pentecost*	Sr Benedicta Ward SLG (2016)
FP181	*Lazarus: Come Out! Reflections on John 11*	Bonnie Thurston (2017)
FP182	*Unknowing & Astonishment: Meditations on Faith for the Long Haul*	Christopher Scott (2018)
FP183	*Pondering, Praying, Preaching: Romans 8*	Bonnie Thurston (2019)
FP184	*Shem`on the Graceful: Discourse on the Solitary Life*	trans. with introd. Mary Hansbury (2020)
FP185	*God Under my Roof: Celtic Songs and Blessings (revised and enlarged edition)*	Esther de Waal (2020)
FP186	*Journeying with the Jesus Prayer*	James. F. Wellington (2020)